This book belongs to

JB 2016

©Tabitha Barnett 2016

©Tabitha Barnett 2016

©Tabitha Barnett 2016

©Tabitha Barnett 2016

©Tabitha Barnett 2016

Thank You for your purchase! I hope you enjoy this book. You can find all of my other books there as well. I have included a sample packet in the following pages from all of my books. I love to hear from you! If you own any of my books, reviews on Amazon are ALWAYS GREATLY APPRECIATED! Amazon reviews are one of the easiest ways to help indy artists like myself. If you have purchased any of of my books, even in PDF format you can leave a review on Amazon as long as you have purchased anything from Amazon, ever (even a free kindle book).

www.amazon.com/author/tabbystangledart

PDFs, Coloring Packs, Tutorials and single pages:
www.sellfy.com/tabbyb

Become a patron for as little as $1 per month to get new fresh coloring pages in your inbox every month!
www.patreon.com/tabbyb

Add me on facebook and like my artist page to stay up to date and get free printables!
www.facebook.com/tabbystangledart

Follow me on twitter:
@tabbyleann

Get some awesome colorable merchandise like tote bags, greeting cards, notebooks and more:
www.redbubble.com/people/tabbyb

Email: tabbystangledart@gmail.com

©Tabitha Barnett 2015 Book: Tangled Dreams

Book: Doodle Dreams

©Tabitha Barnett 2015

Book: Digi-Dreams

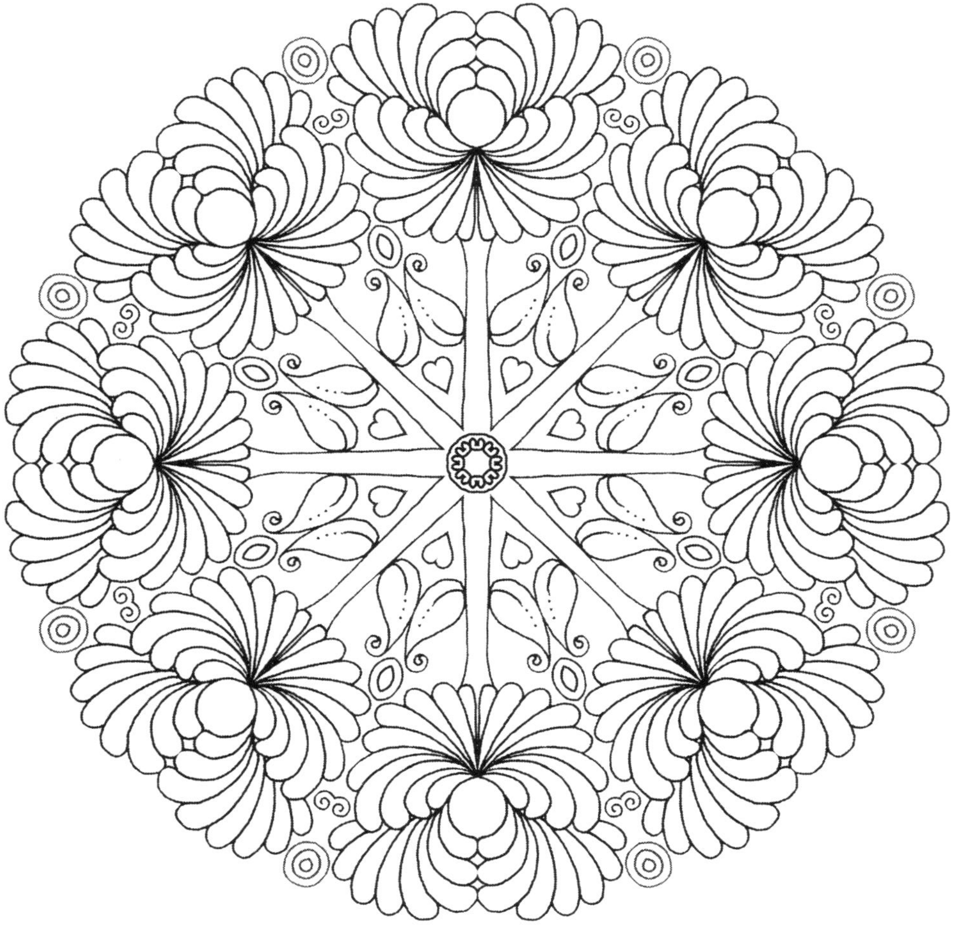

 Book: Majestic Mandalas

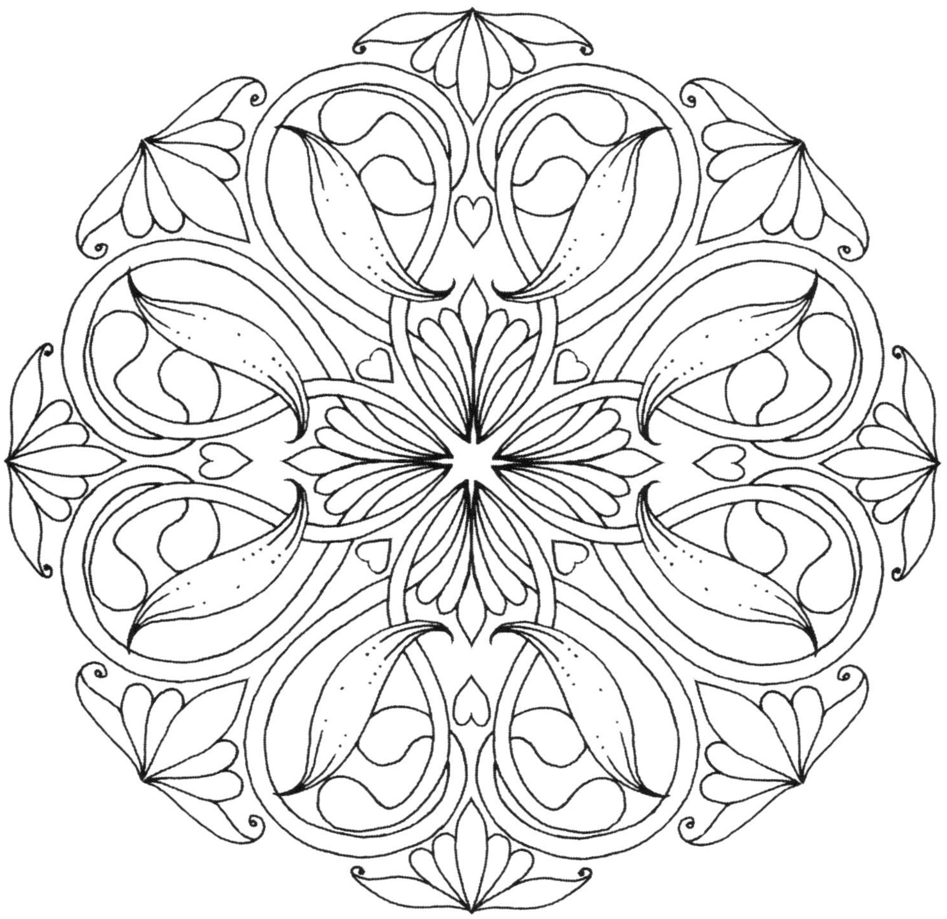

Book: *Tangled Bliss*

Color Chart

Medium: _____ **Brand:** _____

Favorite Color Blends

Made in the USA
Middletown, DE
09 May 2017